How to Build a House

For Sam

First published 2005
Evans Brothers Limited
2A Portman Mansions
Chiltern Street
London W1U 6NR

British Library Cataloguing in Publication Data
Turpin, Nick
        How to build a house. - (Twisters)
        1. Children's stories - Pictorial works
        I. Title
        823.9'2 [J]

ISBN-10: 023753066X
13-digit ISBN (from 1 January 2007) 9780237530662

Printed in China by WKT Company Limited

Series Editor: Nick Turpin
Design: Robert Walster
Production: Jenny Mulvanny
Series Consultant: Gill Matthews

How to Build a House

Nick Turpin
and Barbara Nascimbeni

Evans

Jack wanted to
build a house.

5

"Dad, dig a ditch!"

"Pull!"

9

"Push!"

"Put these here!"

"And another."

Half done.

"We need
more people."

18

20

"Your sister can help us."

"Good work, Dad!"

"Mum must do the last bit."

Finished!

27

"What shall we call it?"

"How about, 'The House That Jack Built!'"

31

Why not try reading another Twisters book?